Follow Me to Palm Springs

By

Pamela Maloof

Contents

Palm Springs

Contents

Contents

Forward

It started over 30 years ago as I moved to the desert for a director position at the Palm Springs Youth Center. I also gave tennis and golf lessons along the way. While teaching, I always loved looking up at the snow-capped mountains of San Jacinto, thinking, "I live in PARADISE!".

My subsequent employment put me in the position of Activity Director. I put on parties for 10 to 400 people, including Mystery Dinners, Ladies Luncheons, and Special Events all over the Coachella Valley.

I always enjoy finding places to go, sites to see, things to do, and outdoor activities for people to participate in while visiting.

Putting my favorite recommendations into one book to share has given me more joy than I could imagine.

Enjoy Paradise!

Pamela Maloof

Pamela Maloof

PALM SPRINGS

The Global Angel Wings Project

Collette Miller created the Global Angel Wings Project in 2012, in the streets of Los Angeles, the City of Angels. They were painted to remind humanity that we are the angels of this earth. They are human sized interactive public art, wings that people take photos with and thus become part of the artwork.

Colette has painted wings globally – Kenya, Australia, Taiwan, France, Cuba, Juarez Mexico and more and many in the USA. Though some are commissioned, and others gifted, the wings themselves are free to the world. Never owned by anyone, not even Colette, though they are of her provenance and her work.

This provides a great location for taking selfies and sets the tone for what downtown Palm springs has to offer.

Located on the north side of the Rowan Hotel at 100 W. Tahquitz Canyon Way , Palm Springs

Forever Marilyn

Welcome to the site of Forever Marilyn, the 26-foot tall, 24,000-pound monumental sculpture created by sculptor Seward Johnson with stainless steel and aluminum. This dramatic sculpture is extremely realistic, especially in the skin tones. Her unique patina involves ten layers of hues with a matte finish, except for the glossy elements of her lips, toenails and the pearlized glaze on her earrings.

Palm Springs is loaded with celebrity statues, but this statue's uniqueness brings to life how star-studded the city really is.

Located next to the Palm Springs Downtown Park in Palm Springs on Museum Way

ISABELLE Optical Illusion Sculpture

This sculpture made of stainless steel and   LED lighting was created by Julian Voss-Andrae in 2018 and is an optical illusion.   It requires you walk completely around it to see the entire illusion.

Located next to The Global Angel Wings Project on the north side of the Rowan Hotel at   100 W. Tahquitz Canyon Way , Palm Springs

Palm Springs Art Museum

Located in the heart of downtown Palm Springs, the Palm Springs Art Museum founded in 1938, features a sophisticated collection of art including pieces by Andy Warhol and Marc Chagall. Spread over the 150,000 square feet, the museum boasts major collections of modern and contemporary art, glass, photography, architecture and design, and Native American and Western art.

The Palm Springs Art Museum is a "cultural oasis" with "wonderful" exhibits. Many also appreciate its small size, adding that it's easy to see everything in an hour or two.

Located at 101 N. Museum Drive in Palm Springs

Le Vallauris Restaurant

You'll feel as if you've entered the home of a French relative who wants nothing better than to make you happy.

The daily offerings are handwritten on a large board brought to your table to stand like artwork on an easel while you make your selections.

Combine that with first-class service, good food, great hospitality and you are in for a real treat.

Le Vallauris is one of my top recommendations to dine al fresco in the Palm Springs area. The beautiful Ficus trees amongst the garden patio provides a stunning ambiance for any special occasion. I always end the evening with their signature Grand Marnier soufflé.

Located at 385 Tahquitz Canyon Way, Palm Springs

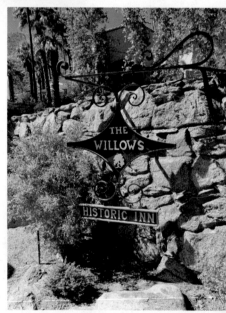

The Willows Historic Inn

What do Clark Gable and Carole Lombard, Joseph P. Kennedy, Marion Davies, Shirley Temple, and Dr. Albert Einstein all have in common? They all have stayed at this opulent hotel in past years.

Built in 1924 this hidden treasure is a dream of peace and serenity and yet is in close proximity to downtown Palm Springs. Today the Willows has been reborn as a private luxury hotel. Treat yourself at least once to this unforgettable enchanted stay.

Located at 412 Tahquitz Canyon Way, Palm Springs

I Love Lucy Bronze Statue

If you were walking downtown Palm Springs in the 1950's, you probably would have walked right past Lucille Ball of the hit TV show "I Love Lucy". Lucy made Palm Springs her weekend home and loved shopping up and down Palm Canyon Drive.

This bronze statue of Lucy Ricardo from "I Love Lucy" was created in 1995 by Emmanuil and Janet Snitkovsky. Sit down next to Lucy for a photo souvenir.

Located at the corner of North Palm Canyon and Tahquitz Canyon Way, Palm Springs

The Walk of Stars in Palm Springs

With over 400 Walk of Stars bearing the names of local celebrities and notable personalities, the Palm Springs Walk of Stars is a must see. These stars are embedded in the sidewalks throughout the downtown Palm Springs area along Palm Canyon Drive, Tahquitz Canyon Way, La Plaza Court and Museum Drive.

Even after walking these sidewalks as many times as I have, I always discover someone new.

Located at 10 North Palm Canyon in Palm Springs

Sonny Bono Statue

Long after singing "I Got You Babe!" with his then wife Cher, Sonny Bono continued to be a giant personality, entertainer, savvy businessman, politician and, of all things, the great Mayor of Palm Springs from 1988 to 1992. He was instrumental in spearheading the creation of the Palm Springs International Film Festival, which is held each year in Bono's memory. It was a great time to live in Palm Springs because he put Palm Springs back on the map.

The bronze sculpture by Emmanuil Snitkovsky depicts Salvatore Phillip "Sonny" Bono seated by the fountain of the Plaza Mercado.

Located at 155 South Palm Canyon in Palm Springs

Tyler's Burgers

Set in a unique 1936 building, Tyler's became a reality in 1996. It was Diana Diamico's dream to re-create the hamburger she fondly remembered from her childhood.

Located in the center of the Mercado Plaza you'll find this fun, casual, local favorite outdoor eating restaurant. Serving All-American classics like burgers, hotdogs, old fashioned malts, homemade potato salad and much more.

Located at 149 S Indian Canyon Dr, Palm Springs

Spencer's Restaurant

Set at the historic Palm Springs Tennis Club, an exclusive gathering place for such celebrities as Katherine Hepburn and Bob Hope since its inception in the 1930s, Spencer's Restaurant is synonymous with the desert's classic style. Elegance and comfortable informality intertwine to accommodate any dining occasion, from a power lunch or private party to a romantic evening for two or Sunday brunch.

The name of the restaurant came from owner Harold Matzner's award-winning 110-pound Siberian husky.

This is one of my top 5 restaurants that has a wonderful old Palm Springs environment set next to the base of the mountains. It's old "Palm Springs" in character with casual classy service providing you a memorable experience.

Located at 701 W Baristo Rd. in Palm Springs

Melvyn's Restaurant &

The Casablanca Lounge

Located on the premises of the legendary Ingleside Inn, Melvyn's is elegantly upbeat and the home of authentic Hollywood glamour. The Casablanca Lounge at Melvyn's is known for its nightly entertainment and the popular Sunday Night Jam Sessions featuring guest musicians and singers.

I have dined at Melvyn's and sat at the Casablanca Lounge for over 20 years. Many drinks sitting at the bar and fond memories of dancing on the dance floor make this one of my "Special" Recommendations.

Located at 200 W Ramon Rd, Palm Springs

Moorten Botanical Garden

The Moorten Botanical Garden and Cactarium is a 1-acre family-owned botanical garden specializing in cacti and other desert plants.

This privately-owned arboretum was created to share the beauty and extraordinary varieties of desert plants.

This is a good, quick excursion while you're in town. It's a small garden but very lovely.

Located at 1701 S. Palm Canyon Dr., Palm Springs

Palm Springs Historical District

Leisurely explore some of the original Palm Springs history at the Village Green Heritage Center while walking through the downtown area. The center consists of the McCallum Adobe (built in 1884), Miss Cornelia White's House (built in 1893), Ruddy's General Store (built in 1930) and the Agua Caliente Cultural Museum.

The center is located on Palm Canyon Drive and is dedicated to those Native Americans and pioneers who first settled the area.

I recommend stopping off at this quaint establishment for a trip down history lane and revisit what it must have been like in the early days of Palm Springs.

Located at 219–221 S. Palm Canyon Drive, Palm Springs

Palm Springs Aerial Tramway

The Palm Springs Aerial Tramway in Palm Springs is the largest rotating aerial tramway in the world. It was opened in September 1963 as a way of getting from the floor of the Coachella Valley to near the top of San Jacinto Peak and was constructed in the rugged Chino Canyon.

Once to the top, you will experience a 30 degree drop in temperature and a breathtaking view. In addition, there are many trails to hike and see.

This is absolutely your best choice to see the entire Coachella Valley.

Located at 1 Tram Way, Palm Springs

Windmill Tours

When driving into Palm Springs from Los Angeles, the first sign you've arrived in the desert is the row upon row of windmills along both sides of the highway.

The Windmill Tours is a top attraction for friends and family to learn about wind energy, how wind turbines work and the history of the Palm Springs Wind Farms. You can actually get up close to these 400 ft high windmills.

Most of us who have come to the desert the first time want to know more about these giant energy machines. The Windmill Tours will provide you answers to all of your questions.

Located at 62950 20th Ave., Palm Springs

Palm Springs Air Museum

The Palm Springs Air Museum, is a non-profit educational institution in Palm Springs. The Museum's mission is to exhibit, educate and eternalize the role of World War II combat aircrafts and the role the pilots and American citizens had in winning the war.

Any history or WWII buff needs to pay this place a visit. It has one of the world's largest collection of flyable WWII planes on site.

Located at 745 N Gene Autry Trail, Palm Springs

Windmill Market

Treat yourself to the "The Best Date Shake in the Palm Springs area" at the Windmill Market.

This is another hidden gem where Palm Springs locals head for Date Shakes.

Thumbs up to this great local store on taste, value and service.

You'll be surprised at how good a date shake can taste.

Located at 17080 N Indian Canyon Dr, North Palm Springs

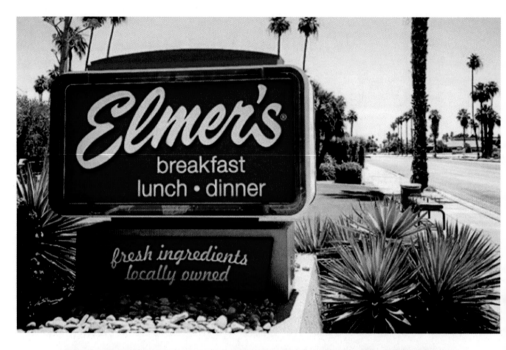

Elmer's Restaurant

One of the most popular items they serve at Elmer's Restaurant is their buttermilk pancakes which are made from scratch from an Elmer family recipe.

Breakfast, Lunch and Dinner have been offered at this same spot for over 30 years.

Generous portions are offered with yummy fresh versions of diner food.

Elmer's restaurant is a great way to start your vacation day right. It will be one of your best stops yet.

Located at 1030 E Palm Canyon Dr, Palm Springs

Counter Reformation Restaurant

This hidden hangout with a speakeasy feel for global wines & bites is located inside the Parker Hotel. The Parker Hotel is situated on 13 acres for you to eat, play and love.

What an adventurous dining experience... Walking through the lobby out the double French doors we were greeted by an associate from the Parker. He kindly walked us over via a hidden pathway to the doorstep of Counter Reformation. And this my friends, is where the magic started. Here you will be mesmerized by the two confessionals in the back. Bar seating and ledge leaning is the rule of thumb.

Located at 4200 E Palm Canyon, Palm Springs

High Bar @ the Rowan Hotel

Unique in the sprawling landscape of Palm Springs, High Bar sits adjacent to the rooftop pool atop seven stories, offering transcendent views alongside impeccable drinks and cool, classy furnishings. With a lush backdrop and a color palette of blues, grays, whites and warm wood tones. The vibe is refreshing and playful by day, yet swank and seductive once the sun sets and the stars emerge overhead. An expansive bar serves up classic and retro cocktails, craft beers from Coachella Valley and crisp wines. Delectable drinks, vivid vistas—it's a no-fail recipe for living the high life.

Located at 100 Tahquitz Canyon Way, Palm Springs

Palm Springs Villagefest

Palm Springs Villagefest happens every Thursday in downtown Palm Springs on world famous Palm Canyon Drive between Amado Road and Baristo Road. October-May 6PM-10PM, Summer Hours: June-September 7PM-10PM.

Enjoy a diverse array of artists, artisans, entertainers, assorted fruits, vegetables, fresh flowers, jewelry, international cuisine, and don't forget the sweets.

Located on Palm Canyon Drive between Armado and Baristo Road, Palm Springs

Cathedral City

Interactive Hot Air Balloon Mural

This mural is meant to be an interactive piece of art that provides the public with a fun opportunity to photograph themselves and share with their friends via social media.

After attending an afternoon movie with my cousins at the Mary Pickford Theater, we walked out to find a great photo opt right outside the door.

Located at 36850 Pickfair St, Cathedral City

Rancho Mirage

Ritz-Carlton

Highlighted by spectacular views from its dramatic cliff-side setting, the Ritz-Carlton offers many ways of enjoying a stay. From the holistic spa to the Club Lounge, this place offers an elevated experience of a lifetime.

Honestly, I just love sitting in the outside patio area watching the sun go down and the skylight come up. I'm sure you will too.

Located at the Ritz-Carlton, 68900 Frank Sinatra Dr, Rancho Mirage

Sunnylands Center and Gardens

Sunnylands Center & Gardens offers visitors a beautiful, tranquil, and environmentally sustainable space to learn about Ambassadors Walter and Leonore Annenberg, their history at Sunnylands, the famous people who visited, and the contemporary retreat program. Guests can watch a film, enjoy art exhibitions, explore walking trails through the 9-acre gardens, purchase items in the gift shop, or enjoy light lunch items in the café. A variety of free wellness programs and activities are offered Nov. through April (closed June-September). Admission and parking are free. Tours of the historic midcentury modern home are available with advance ticket purchase.

After taking a bird walk tour, there is nothing better than sitting outside the café enjoying a French press pot of coffee and a homemade turkey sandwich. This is a piece of heaven in the desert. This is another one of my top 5 places to see.

Located at 37977 Bob Hope Dr, Rancho Mirage

Palm Desert

Keedy's Fountain & Grill

A true diner with a laid-back 1950s American feel, coupled with the best comfort food in Palm Desert. Keedy's is a warm nostalgic place to catch up with friends. Come for a hearty breakfast with a cup of Joe or a homestyle burger with a real milkshake.

Definitely a local favorite in Palm Desert. It reminds me of sitting at the soda fountain bar sipping on a milkshake with my dad. I highly recommend trying it for breakfast or lunch.

Located at 73-633 Hwy-111, Palm Desert

Jillian's

Whether you choose one of the distinctive dining rooms or the inviting outdoor courtyard, enchanting garden or private terrace, every detail will be attended to, every need met. Superb eclectic cuisine is graciously served in this extraordinary atmosphere.

By far one of the most intimate, romantic and inviting dining places in Palm Desert. Reserve a table for your perfect night out.

Located at 74155 El Paseo, Palm Desert

The Living Desert Zoo & Gardens

The Living Desert Zoo and Gardens is a non-profit zoo and desert botanical garden located in Palm Desert. Home to over 500 animals representing over 150 species, the Living Desert welcomes over 500,000 visitors annually. But don't worry there is plenty of space to walk around and see everything.

Feeding the giraffes is a highlight for both kids and adults. There are many other new exhibits including the new Rhino Savanna and Australian Adventures. You will be pleasantly surprised by the size of this zoo. Another one of my top picks.

Located at 47900 Portola Ave, Palm Desert

Terrace Restaurant

at Desert Willow

Unwind on the spacious outdoor patio offering breathtaking views of the sun setting over Firecliff hole 9 and 18. This is one of the most scenic outdoor dining venues in Palm Desert.

My girlfriends and I love playing golf here. Afterwards we relax at the Terrace Restaurant and collect our winnings.

Located at 38-995 Desert Willow Dr, Palm Desert

Vista Point Lookout

A fun place to stop on your way up or down Hwy 74 Pines to Palms switchbacks just outside of Palm Desert.

Best viewing opportunities are at dusk or at night.

Located on Hwy 74 Pines to Palms Hwy, Palm Desert

Public Art Exhibit on El Paseo

The Biennial El Paseo Exhibition brings together unique works of art from local, national, and international artists for display on the median along the upscale El Paseo shopping district.

Download the app **Otocast**, search for "El Paseo" and you will hear the sculptor speak about their art pieces. Shopping down El Paseo is a must, but the art exhibits are like icing on the cake.

Located on El Paseo, Palm Desert

Si Bon

Si Bon welcomes you with a warm and stylish European atmosphere. This comfortable, charming bistro makes you feel as if you are traveling abroad.

Choose from a variety of Belgian-inspired dishes, including waffles, sandwiches, seafood and desserts.

Delicious waffles are incorporated into almost every dish. A delightfully different breakfast, lunch or dinner awaits you here. An exciting brunch menu is also served on the weekends.

Located on 40101 Monterey Ave., Rancho Mirage

il Corso Restaurant - Palm Desert

Il Corso offers genuine Italian hospitality, authentic Italian dishes like homemade pasta, gourmet wood oven pizza, seafood and roasted leg of veal.

Chef Mario also brings out nightly specials from all over Italy like the world's best gnocchi, incredible meat dishes, and Italian-style martinis with a wonderful variety of desserts and fresh salads.

I have spent many afternoons and evenings having intimate dining experiences. The service, ambiance and taste always makes me feel like I'm on vacation in Italy again. One of my Top 5 favorites in the desert.

Located at 73520 El Paseo, Palm Desert

Indian Wells

Pink Cabana at the Sands Hotel

As the first designer boutique hotel in the prominent and exclusive community of Indian Wells, the Pink Cabana has received world-renowned accolades from Condé Nast Traveler, LA Times, Forbes, and many others. Chef Ethan Brown creates an ingredient-driven menu featuring Mediterranean cuisine with a Moroccan influence.

A few steps from the pool and pink everything! I love the retro chic vibe. It is a gorgeous bar and restaurant you should try. The food and décor are as glamorous as they are trendy.

Located at 44-985 Province Way, Indian Wells

La Quinta

La Quinta Resort & Club

Set on 45 lush acres of vibrantly-colored gardens and pathways, La Quinta Resort offers hacienda-style casitas and suites clustered around 41 pools.

The views of the Santa Rosa mountains surrounding the resort are incredible. In some areas you think you are looking at a painting.

I highly recommend strolling around the La Quinta Resort and Club taking in the beautiful flowers, the water features and the ambiance of this luxury resort.

Located at 49-499 Eisenhower Dr, La Quinta

Ernie's Bar Grill

Ernie's is a great place to eat, drink and enjoy the "PGA West" panoramic view of the 18th hole.

Try and catch a table on the outdoor patio during a sunset or a full moon as it is a beautiful and unforgettable experience with the expansive views of the golf course and desert.

Located at 56-150 PGA Blvd, La Quinta

Big Metal Roadrunner

A larger-than-life music loving bird has found a nest in La Quinta. The giant roadrunner that made its debut at the Coachella Music Festival has flown a few miles west and landed in the middle of a traffic circle.

Drive around this sculpture while seeing the sites in La Quinta.

Located at Jefferson Street & Avenue 52, La Quinta

Pete's Grill at Pete Dye Clubhouse

A tribute to the famed golf course architect who designed both courses, the Pete Dye Clubhouse boasts stunning views from the Mountains and Dunes courses nestled against the Santa Rosa Mountain Range. The spacious clubhouse has an inviting lounge, and the perfect place to start and end your game.

I come here to enjoy another spectacular view of the panoramic mountains while enjoying a delicious hamburger and fries.

Located at 50200 Avenida Vista Bonita, La Quinta

Lavender Bistro

"The Best Kept Secret in La Quinta" is Lavender Bistro. And you probably can guess that the primary color for the décor is "lavender". Aside from the beautiful outdoor seating under a multitude of Ficus trees or tucked away cabanas, the food is sensational. They combine the finest meats and seafood with the freshest organic ingredients to create unforgettable dishes.

The ambiance is magical, and the food is superb.

Located at 78-073 Calle Barcelona, La Quinta

Indio

Café at Shields

Situated on Shields Date Garden's exclusive and historical venue, Café at Shields opened its doors in October of 2010 offering a unique and impressive atmosphere for local and visiting diners alike.

This place is a true hidden gem. In addition to the outdoor café, there is an extensive unique gift shop, a beautiful garden to stroll through, and a theater where you can watch the film "Sex Life of a Date".

Save room after a date-inspired breakfast or lunch for a "World Famous" Shield's Date Shake at the original counter set up in the 1960's.

Located at 80225 CA Hwy -111 in Indio

Tack Room Tavern

Located at the beautiful Empire Polo Club in the City of Festivals (Indio), you'll find the Tack Room Tavern, offering a fun and casual dining experience immersed in the history of the equestrian community since 1987. You can enjoy classic American cuisine, fresh cocktails and live entertainment year-round.

Inside this favorite local spot, you'll find several leather saddle stools to sit in while enjoying great food, drinks and a tavern atmosphere.

Located at 81800 Avenue 51 in Indio

ELDORADO POLO

POLO

ELDORADO POLO CLUB
ANTELOPE   JR   ALPHA OMEGA

PERIOD

4   4   2

0:00

P BOSSON   1   1 N WERENBERG
L SCHROEBELEN   2 V RIVKIN
G PALMER   3   3 L FLOCCARI
B BOSSON   4   4 ELRIGHT

POLO ASSN.
SINCE 1890

65
YEARS
SINCE 1957

2022

Eldorado Polo Club

With expansive mountain views at the east end of the Coachella Valley, Eldorado Polo Club is a paradise for top polo players from around the world. Since 1957, the club has offered the best conditions to play "the sport of kings" every Sunday during the winter months January through March

My favorite movie is "Pretty Woman" and the Eldorado Polo Club allows tailgating, half time divot stomping, and sipping champagne just like in the movie.

Located at 81800 Avenue 51 in Indio

El Mexicali Cafe

Authentic Mexican food is only served here utilizing secret family recipes. It may be a small establishment, but the food and staff are amazing. The "Chiles Gueritos" are a popular local favorite featuring shrimp stuffed yellow peppers topped with mayo and soy sauce. (who knew?). The "Shake, Rattle, and Roll" of the trains passing by on the train tracks behind this restaurant is also something you'll never forget! My fav in the desert.

Located at 82720 Indio Blvd, Indio

Coachella Valley History Museum

The Coachella Valley History Museum is committed to preserving, sharing and interpreting the history of the Coachella Valley. It was established in 1965.

This is a delightful off the path small local museum worth a visit.

It's worth your while to stop by if you love learning about farming, dates and the history of the Coachella Valley including the nearby Salton Sea.

Located at 82616 Miles Ave, Indio

TKB Bakery & Deli

TKB (short for The Kids Business) has come a long way from its humble beginnings in the kitchen of the Sippel family. TKB started out in 1991 when the three Sippel siblings would go door-to-door to sell their mom's cookie dough. The business has continued to grow as it became renowned for its tasty sandwiches, even being named the #1 in Yelp's 100 Places to Eat list for 2018.

Recently renovated, the variety of large sandwiches speaks for themselves. Unbelievably delicious with funky names like Hangover, Dirty Riverside and Sexy Italian will leave you craving to try them all.

Located at 45334 Golf Center Pkwy, Indio

Surrounding Areas

Cabazon Dinosaurs

Cabazon Dinosaurs, formerly Claude Bell's Dinosaurs, is a roadside attraction in Cabazon featuring two enormous, steel-and-concrete dinosaurs named Dinny the Dinosaur and Mr. Rex. Located just west of Palm Springs, the 150-foot-long *Brontosaurus* and the 65-foot-tall *Tyrannosaurus rex* are visible from the freeway to travelers passing by on Southern California's Interstate 10. The roadside dinosaurs are best known for their appearance in the film *Pee-wee's Big Adventure* (1985).

Located at 50770 Seminole Dr, Cabazon

General George S. Patton Memorial Museum

The General George S. Patton Memorial Museum, in Chiriaco Summit is a museum erected in tribute to General George S. Patton on the site of the entrance of Camp Young, part of the Desert Training Center of World War II.

Approximately 30 minutes from Indio, this is a great place for looking at the history of General Patton and military memorabilia of WWI and WWII. There are many different tanks and military equipment on the property to take a few great selfies.

Located at 62510 Chiriaco Rd, Chiriaco Summit

Cabot Pueblo Museum

Cabot's Pueblo Museum is an American historic house museum located in Desert Hot Springs and built by Cabot Yerxa, an early pioneer of the Colorado Desert. This museum is such a treasure offering a lot of history, a self guided phone tour and lots of great photo ops.

Located at 67616 Desert View Ave, Desert Hot Springs

Joshua Tree National Park

Named for the region's twisted, bristled Joshua Trees, two distinct desert ecosystems, the Mojave and the Colorado, come together. Dark night skies, a rich cultural history, and surreal geologic features add to the wonder of this vast wilderness in southern California.   Activities include camping, hiking, photography, rock climbing and simply enjoying the serene desert scenery.

So beautiful and vast. There is a lot to do here if you love outdoors. The dark night skies let you see the stars which is so worth it. I recently saw the Milky Way for the first time since I was a kid.

Located at 74485 National Park Drive, 29 Palms

Gubler Orchid Farm

The Gubler family has loved and grown orchids for four generations.

Gubler Orchids has a reputation as one of the top-quality orchid growers in the world.

This will be a surprising oasis and the highlight of your trip. Amazing orchids with so many varieties. You will not leave here empty handed.

Located at 2200 Belfield Blvd, Landers

Coachella Valley Preserve

Starting from the Visitors Center, the Coachella Valley Preserve includes a mile-long trail that winds past pools containing endangered desert pupfish. The Coachella Valley fringe-toed lizard depends on this unusual blow sand desert for survival, and "swims" through the sand to escape predators or summer heat on the desert surface.

Nestled in seemingly the middle of nowhere, this magical oasis springs up right on the San Andreas fault line. The oasis provides gorgeous views, lovely shade, great bird watching and fantastic photo ops. Truly a must see.

Located at 29200 Thousand Palms Canyon Rd, Thousand Palms

Oasis Date Shake and Gardens

Established in 1912, Oasis Date Gardens is one of the oldest date gardens in the Coachella Valley. The 175-acre-producing ranch harvests over 15 different date varieties all carefully grown organic!

Visit the store and experience another "world-famous" date shake. Then you make the decision which date shake is "world famous".

Located at 59-111 Grapefruit Blvd, Thermal

Pappy and Harriet's in Pioneertown Palace

Pappy & Harriet's Pioneertown Palace is a honky - tonk, barbecue food restaurant and live music venue incorporated within Pioneertown near Joshua Tree National Park.

Pioneertown, founded in 1946 by a group of Hollywood investors, is a historical old west mining town with historical buildings galore used as a film set.

Really iconic place to visit, have some good barbecue food and look around.

Located at 53688 Pioneertown Rd, Pioneertown

La Copine Restaurant

Out of the stark upper desert sprung this unbelievably incredible restaurant called La Copine. This place is impressive.

Great place to enjoy a WOW meal. The food is fresh, consistent, delicious and full of love. Highly recommend the trip. Reservations are highly recommended. Worth the wait.

Located at 848 Old Woman Springs Rd, Yucca Valley

Local Casinos

Agua Caliente Casino Palm Springs
401 E. Amado Rd, Palm Springs

Agua Caliente Casino Rancho Mirage
32250 Bob Hope Dr, Rancho Mirage

Agua Caliente Casino Cathedral City
68960 E Palm Canyon Dr, Cathedral City

Augustine Casino
84001 Avenue 54, Coachella

Fantasy Springs Resort Casino
84245 Indio Springs Pkwy, Indio

Spotlight 29 Casino
46200 Harrison Pl, Coachella

Local Hiking

Andreas Canyon Trail
Drive to the end of South Palm Canyon Drive, Palm Springs

Araby Trail
Southridge Drive, Palm Springs

Joshua Tree National Park
There are multiple entrances to the Park

Murray Canyon Trail
2019 E. Murray, Palm Springs

Palm Springs Aerial Tramway Hiking
1 Tramway, Palm Springs

Palm Springs Museum Trail
Behind 101 N Museum Dr, Palm Springs

Thousand Palms Oasis Preserve
29200 Thousand Palms Canyon Rd, Thousand Palms

Bump and Grind Trail
72440 Painters Path, Palm Desert, CA, 92260

Local Signature Events

January
AMEX Golf Tournament
Palm Springs International Film Festival

February
Modernism Week

March
BNP Paribas Open Tennis Tournament
La Quinta Art Celebration
Fashion Week El Paseo

April
Coachella Valley Music and Arts Festival
Stagecoach Country Music Festival
White Party

June
Palm Springs International Short Film Festival

August
Splash House

September
Cinema Diverse

October
Joshua Tree Music Festival

November
Greater Palm Springs Pride
Hot Air Balloon Festival and Food Truck Fiesta

December
International Tamale Festival
Holiday Parade in Palm Springs

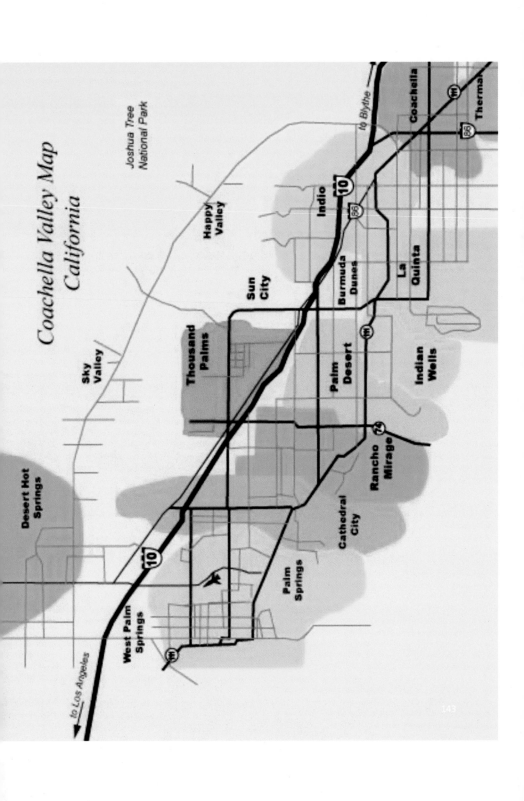

Coachella Valley Map
California

Made in the USA
Coppell, TX
20 July 2023

19390254R00086